KU-589-003

Corvina Kiadó

Introduction et choix d'œuvres du peintre par András Székely

Introduction and selection of paintings by András Székely

Einleitung und Bildauswahl von András Székely

Mihály Munkácsy

CONTROL DATA ARTS

a service of
CONTROL DATA CORPORATION

St. Paul, Minnesota
1981

Traduit par Kató Vargyas
Les photographies des tableaux conservés en
Hongrie sont dues à Alfréd Schiller : les photographies des œuvres conservées à l'étranger nous
ont été gracieusement concédées
par les différentes collections.
Maquette par István Faragó

Translated by Zsuzsa Béres
The photographs of the pictures in Hungarian
collections were made by Alfréd Schiller, the others
were reproduced by courtesy of the foreign
collections.
Design by István Faragó

Übertragen von Géza Engl
Die Fotos der in Ungarn befindlichen Bilder sind
von Alfréd Schiller; die im Ausland befindlichen
reproduzieren wir dank der Gefälligkeit der
betreffenden Sammlungen.
Gestaltung von István Faragó

Library of Congress Cataloging in Publication Data

Munkácsy, Mihály, 1844-1900.
  Mihály Munkácsy.

  Translation of Munkácsy Mihály.
  Text in English, French, and German.
  1. Munkácsy, Mihály, 1844-1900. I. Székely, András,
fl. 1972-
ND522.5.M8A4   1980   759.39   80-21413
ISBN 0-89893-168-1

Copyright © 1980 András Székely

All rights reserved

Printed and bound in Hungary
Corvina Press, Budapest, Hungary

Introduction

Un grand romancier réaliste hongrois du xxᵉ siècle, Zsigmond Móricz, a écrit en 1910 un petit livre sur la carrière du peintre Mihály Munkácsy, pour une série de poche destinée aux jeunes ouvriers. Cette brève esquisse se termine par ces mots : « Le petit orphelin de Munkács, abandonné, en butte à tant de maux, a pris le chemin de la vie sans un sou en poche. Et quand le grand artiste descendit au tombeau, toute l'humanité le pleura. Et ces deux-là n'étaient qu'une seule et même personne. C'est le héros fabuleux de notre monde d'aujourd'hui ! Et cette voie est ouverte à tous les jeunes. »

On a l'impression de lire l'histoire d'une carrière, romantique et édulcorée. Même l'écrivain réaliste, qui connaît bien les profondeurs de la vie, a été trahi par son sens des proportions. Lui aussi a peint l'image qui s'était déjà imprimée dans la conscience générale des Hongrois sur l'artiste arrivé. C'est un petit orphelin, apprenti menuisier, qui à Paris possédera des hôtels particuliers, et dont les tableaux religieux sont montrés au public, avec entrée payante, dans les grandes villes d'Europe. Dont la femme est baronne. Qui prend part aux festivités somptueuses du millénaire en Hongrie, en un costume de parade magnifique et presque historique, et dont le cortège funèbre réunira d'innombrables représentants des différentes associations d'artistes. Et pourtant, ce n'était qu'un petit apprenti menuisier, le « héros fabuleux de notre monde d'aujourd'hui »...

Le romancier a l'excuse qu'en ce temps-là il était presque impossible à Budapest d'apprécier l'art de ce peintre considéré comme le plus grand des peintres hongrois. Ses œuvres célèbres, souvent de dimensions énormes, récompensées de médailles d'or, étaient dispersées dans différentes collections du monde : *le Dernier Jour d'un condamné* était à Boston, *le Mont de Piété* et *Milton* à New York, *la Mort de Mozart* à Detroit, *le Héros du village* à Cologne, *le Christ au prétoire* et *le Calvaire* à Philadelphie, et le tableau *A l'atelier*, si pittoresque d'après les reproductions, avait également échoué en Amérique ; malheureusement, nous ne savons plus aujourd'hui où il se trouve... L'écrivain n'avait pu voir que des « héliogravures » dans le livre de l'ancien secrétaire de l'artiste, publié en 1898. C'est là qu'il avait pu lire l'autobiographie de Munkácsy ; d'autre part, des études consacrées à l'artiste lui avaient fait connaître quelques épisodes de sa vie, et il avait encore pu voir au Musée des Beaux-Arts de Budapest quelques tableaux, répliques en dimensions réduites : *le Dernier Jour d'un condamné*, avec deux personnages, *la Femme aux fagots*, le *Chemin poussiéreux*, les *Adieux*, *la Femme à la baratte*, le *Troupeau au pâturage*, l'*Allée*, et bien d'autres toiles caractéristiques de Munkácsy, étaient

Introduction

A twentieth century Hungarian novelist, Zsigmond Móricz, wrote a short serial about the career of Mihály Munkácsy. It appeared in a popular series which was prepared for the working class youth. The brief sketch ended as follows: "This small orphan from Munkács started out in the world with nothing. Although born deserted and seemingly amidst a sea of troubles he died as a great artist mourned by the whole of humanity. It is a modern fairytale of success and it is difficult to imagine that his birth and death are linked in any way. It is a success story open to every young man."

His story was one of "rags to riches". His career was both magnificent and sentimental. This is the impression we get from the above passage. This was also the image formed in the mind of the Hungarian public at the beginning of the century. An experienced writer, perhaps deserted by his sense of proportion who was well acquainted with the realities of life, could offer no alternative view. Although Munkácsy started out as an orphan and carpenter's apprentice he became the owner of Parisian mansions. People paid to see his religious pictures which were exhibited in the great cities of Europe. His wife was a baroness, and at the magnificent festivities marking Hungary's millennium he was seen wearing a splendid historical costume. At his death his funeral was attended by endless lines of mourners, including representatives from the world of art and commerce. He started life humbly and ended it heroically.

It must be understood, however, in defence of the novelist, that Munkácsy's famous works were in various collections all over the world. It was, consequently, difficult to judge just how great a Hungarian artist he was: *The Condemned Cell* was in Boston; *The Pawnbroker's Shop* and *Milton* were in New York; *The Death of Mozart* was in Detroit; *The Village Hero* was in Cologne, and *Christ before Pilate* and *Golgotha* were in Philadelphia. *In the Studio* was, judging from its reproductions, very picturesque. It was taken to the United States and its exact whereabouts are unknown even today.

The novelist had access only to "photoprints" from a book written in 1898 by the painter's former secretary. In this work he was also able to read Munkácsy's autobiography. The secretary wrote a second book in 1907 which produced a few anecdote-like episodes. Móricz was also able to inspect reproductions of *The Condemned Cell*, and *The Village Hero* which, although reduced in size, had come into the possession of the Museum of Fine Arts in Budapest. Only *Lint Makers*, *Tramps of the Night* and the two-figured condemned cell scene, known as *The Condemned*, could be seen in the original. The paintings *Woman Carrying*

Einleitung

Ein prominenter ungarischer Erzähler realistischer Richtung, Zsigmond Móricz, schrieb 1910 ein bescheidenes Büchlein über Mihály Munkácsy, es sollte in einer populären Reihe für junge Arbeiter erscheinen. Die kurze Lebensbeschreibung endete mit diesem Satz: „Der kleine Waisenknabe aus Munkács trat den Weg ins Leben einsam und verlassen, unter tausend Schwierigkeiten und Nöten an. Und ein sehr, sehr großer Künstler stieg von der ganzen Menschheit betrauert ins Grab. Die beiden, der Waisenknabe und der große Künstler, waren ein und dieselbe Person. Ein Märchenheld unserer Zeit. Und dieser Weg steht jedem Jüngling offen."

Man glaubt die romantisch-süßliche Geschichte einer Karriere zu lesen: selbst den realistischen Schriftsteller hat diesmal sein Gefühl für richtige Proportionen betrogen. Auch er konnte nur dasjenige Bild vermitteln, das sich im allgemeinen Bewußtsein der Ungarn am Anfang des Jahrhunderts über den erfolgreichen Künstler festgesetzt hatte. Ein kleiner Waisenknabe, ein Tischlerlehrling, der es zum Besitzer Pariser Paläste brachte, dessen religiöse Gemälde gegen Eintrittsgebühr in den europäischen Großstädten gezeigt wurden, der die Witwe eines Barons zur Frau hatte und der 1896 in seinem großartigen historischen Galaanzug an den glänzenden Festen des tausendjährigen Ungarns teilnehmen konnte. Sein Begräbnis war ein nationaler Trauertag, unabsehbare Mengen, Künstlervereine, Gewerkschaften gaben ihm das letzte Geleit. Und doch brachte man nur einen kleinen Tischlerlehrling zu Grabe, allerdings einen „Märchenhelden unserer Zeit"...

Zur Entschuldigung von Zsigmond Móricz soll angeführt werden, daß man sich damals in Budapest kaum einen Begriff davon machen konnte, wie eigentlich die Kunst des ungarischen Malers, der als der Größte gefeiert wurde, war. Die berühmten, mit Goldmedaillen prämierten und zum Teil riesengroßen Gemälde befanden sich in den bedeutendsten Sammlungen der Welt: „Der letzte Tag eines Verurteilten" in Boston, „Leihhaus" und „Milton" in New York, „Mozarts Tod" in Detroit, „Der Dorfheld" in Köln, „Christus vor Pilatus" und „Kreuzigung" in Philadelphia und das Bild „Im Atelier", nach den Reproduktionen ein recht malerisches Stück, gelangte ebenfalls nach Amerika und ist seitdem leider verschollen.

Der Schriftsteller hatte wohl nichts als Lichtdrucke im Buch des vormaligen Sekretärs des Meisters gesehen, das 1898 erschienen war. Eben da mochte er Munkácsys Autobiographie gelesen und aus anderen Veröffentlichungen wohl auch einige gefällige Episoden erfahren und das eine oder andere von den in

gardés, en 1910 encore, dans des collections particulières, ou faisaient partie de la collection de Madame Munkácsy, récemment cédée à l'État hongrois, sous la condition qu'un monument serait dressé en l'honneur de l'artiste et qu'une monographie lui serait consacrée.

L'esprit public hongrois considère Munkácsy comme le plus grand des peintres de Hongrie, d'après ses tableaux religieux tant de fois reproduits, les anecdotes sur ses hôtels particuliers de Paris, et des mémoires romanesques au ton sentimental. Même aujourd'hui, cette grandeur a en Hongrie une valeur d'axiome. Il n'est donc pas étonnant qu'en « s'attaquant » à Munkácsy vers 1920, le jeune chercheur Lajos Fülep ait provoqué une vive discussion dans l'opinion publique. Partisan convaincu de l'art moderne, cet historien de l'art avait pour ainsi dire de la peine à voir qu'il existait dans le Paris des années 1870 un grand talent hongrois, capable de lutter pour l'avant-garde de l'époque, mais qui s'était rangé parmi les adversaires de l'impressionnisme, et malgré ses succès momentanés s'était ainsi exclu de la liste de ceux à qui la postérité accorde le plus d'estime... « Il séjournait à Paris en 1867 et il n'avait compris ni Courbet ni Manet, ni ce que ces deux hommes signifiaient pour les successeurs, il ne s'était pas rallié à eux... ne pas même voir Manet, Renoir et Cézanne ! » — s'exclame avec douleur Lajos Fülep.

Que serait-il arrivé si Munkácsy avait adhéré vers 1875 aux impressionnistes, encore méprisés et en proie à des soucis matériels ? (Les deux toiles intitulées *Chemin poussiéreux* montrent que cette idée n'était pas si éloignée de lui.) Il serait probablement mort de faim. Peut-être figurerait-il dans l'index des noms de telle ou telle monographie, parmi des figurants négligeables, comme József Rippl-Rónai, le « nabi » hongrois, coté jusqu'à nos jours bien au-dessous de sa valeur dans la littérature d'histoire de l'art. Lajos Fülep a toujours cité l'art de ce dernier comme un exemple à suivre par les contemporains, et, sans le dire, il « recommandait » à Munkácsy la voie suivie par lui. Il est à noter qu'au début de sa carrière, Rippl-Rónai était l'aide de Munkácsy à Paris, et c'est auprès de lui qu'il avait pu assimiler tout ce à quoi il avait par la suite tourné le dos ! Cependant, derrière Munkácsy, il n'y avait pas de maître pour lui donner des directives, ni même, ce qui est d'une grande importance, une formation académique suffisamment longue à Munich. Dans ce sens, Munkácsy était vraiment un « selfmade man », un héros fabuleux du capitalisme en essor. Ses successeurs avaient pu s'instruire grâce à son œuvre ; mais lui n'avait eu qu'un peintre provincial anonyme pour l'engager dans la voie de l'art qui devait lui valoir tant de succès. Quant à sa propre opinion sur ses succès, c'est une toute autre question. Il est évident qu'en premier lieu il s'en réjouissait, il avait plaisir à lire les articles des journaux sur les bals, les réceptions offerts dans son hôtel par-

Faggots, Dusty Road, Farewell, Woman Churning, Grazing Cattle, Avenue and many other typical Munkácsy pictures were still, in 1910, owned by private collectors. On the conditions that a memorial statue be raised and a monograph be written about her husband, Mrs. Munkácsy gave her collection to the Hungarian State Archives.

On the basis of the frequently reproduced ·religious paintings, on the anecdotes about his Paris palaces and his easy-flowing, somewhat sentimental autobiography the Hungarians accepted Munkácsy as the greatest Hungarian painter. Today, in Hungary, this in fact, is regarded as axiomatic! It was little wonder that when Lajos Fülep attacked Munkácsy in the 1920s, the young scholar's writings became the source of a great public controversy. This art historian fought resolutely for the benefit of modern art. While he acknowledged Munkácsy's talent, he thought it unworthy of a talented artist not to have become an advocate of avant-garde art when his support was vital and possible. Indeed, Munkácsy in the Paris of the 1880s joined the enemies of the Impressionism. Although he was successful in his time, it was this mistake that subsequently excluded him from those held in great esteem by posterity. In 1867 he visited Paris. He neither comprehended nor identified himself with Manet. It was this disregard, especially when we consider how much these men meant to later generations that caused Lajos Fülep to lament —"to not even notice Manet, Renoir and Cézanne !"

The Impressionists in 1878 were still despised and they had to struggle to make ends meet. What would have happened if Munkácsy had joined them? (His two *Dusty Road* pictures prove that this thought had crossed his mind.) He would probably have starved. Perhaps he would have been indicated in one or two large monographs as a minor artist. This is exemplified by comparing him with József Rippl-Rónai, another Hungarian, who is grossly undervalued by professional and international artistic opinion. Lajos Fülep himself suggested that his art should be an example to his contemporaries. He even made overtones that here there was much in store for Munkácsy himself. It should also be said that at the beginning of his career József Rippl-Rónai was Munkácsy's assistant in Paris. He later, however, turned his back on everything that he had learned from Munkácsy perhaps as a result of his academic training in Munich. Munkácsy had neither a guiding master nor an academic training. In this sense he really was self-made: a pathfinder in a flourishing economic age. While Munkácsy's followers learned a lot from him, he himself was taught by Elek Szamossy, an unknown provincial painter.

Just how he saw his own success, however, is another matter. It is fairly obvious that on the whole he was happy with it. He enjoyed the

verkleinertem Maßstab reproduzierten großen Gemälde gesehen haben : Varianten der Gemälde „Der letzte Tag eines Verurteilten" und „Der Dorfheld". Lediglich die „Scharpiezupferinnen" und die „Nächtlichen Vagabunden" waren in Ungarn im Original zu sehen sowie die unter dem Titel „Der Verurteilte" bekannte zweifigurige Variante des Werkes „Der letzte Tag eines Verurteilten". „Reisigtragende Frau" „Staubiger Weg" („Fahrt auf der Pußta"), „Abschied", „Frau beim Buttern", „Weidende Herde", „Allee" und noch viele andere charakteristische Bilder Munkácsys waren 1910 noch in Privatsammlungen oder erst vor kurzem aus der Sammlung Frau Munkácsys in den Besitz des ungarischen Staates übergegangen, mit der Bedingung, dem Maler ein Denkmal zu errichten und eine Monographie über seine Kunst schreiben zu lassen.

So verdankte denn Munkácsy seinen Platz als größter ungarischer Maler den vielmals reproduzierten religiösen Bildern, den Anekdoten aus den Pariser Palästen und der stellenweise etwas sentimental ausgeschmückten Autobiographie. Doch es galt –. eigentlich gilt auch heute noch – als Axiom: Munkácsy ist der größte ungarische Maler. Kein Wunder also, daß, als der junge Kunsthistoriker Lajos Fülep um 1920 eine Attacke gegen Munkácsy ritt, er einen wahren Sturm in der öffentlichen Meinung erregte. Der für den Sieg der modernen Kunst mutig kämpfende Fülep bedauerte es von ganzem Herzen, daß es einen solchen hochbegabten ungarischen Künstler im Paris der siebziger Jahre gab, der sehr wohl als ein Vorkämpfer der damaligen Avantgarde hätte gelten können, stattdessen, gestützt auf seine beispiellosen Erfolge, sich den Feinden der Impressionisten anschloß und sich dadurch selbst von der Liste der durch das 20. Jahrhundert am höchsten geschätzten Künstler strich. „Er war 1867 in Paris gewesen, ohne von Courbet und Manet und von all dem, was die beiden für die Nachwelt bedeuteten, etwas verstanden und sich mit ihnen identifiziert zu haben... einen Manet, einen Renoir und einen Cézanne einfach übersehend..." klagte Lajos Fülep.

Was wäre geschehen, wenn Munkácsy sich den Impressionisten, die um 1875 noch kaum beachtet, mit materiellen Sorgen zu kämpfen hatten, angeschlossen hätte? (Die beiden Varianten von „Staubiger Weg" oder „Fahrt auf der Pußta" bezeugen, daß der Gedanke ihm doch nicht ganz fremd war.) Höchstwahrscheinlich wäre er verhungert. Oder er stünde im besten Falle im Namensregister einer großen Monographie unter den weniger bedeutenden Nebenpersonen, etwa wie József Rippl-Rónai, der Ungar der „Nabis", der in der internationalen Fachliteratur auch heute noch weit unter seiner Bedeutung gewürdigt wird. Fülep, der die Kunst Rippl-Rónais seinen Zeitgenossen immer als das zu befolgende Beispiel empfahl, hätte Munkácsy sicherlich den Weg zugedacht, den Rippl-Rónai ging. Es tut gut, daran

ticulier de Paris. Cependant, sur l'immense panneau de plafond du Kunsthistorisches Museum à Vienne, *l'Apothéose de la Renaissance*, son autoportrait placé parmi ceux des grands artistes jette autour de lui des coups d'œil effarés. C'est « le portrait d'un homme qui se considère presque avec ironie » — lit-on dans la monographie fondamentale sur Munkácsy. Serait-ce vraiment de l'ironie ? Ou une confession involontaire ? En tout cas, il recèle la peur d'un échec. Pendant toute sa vie, **Munkácsy** n'avait pas pu se défaire d'un certain état de *stress* : qu'adviendrait-il si, un beau jour, il se réveillait et voyait que la médaille d'or du Salon gagnée à l'âge de vingt-six ans, et toute la gloire, toute la fortune si facilement acquises n'étaient que le rêve d'un petit apprenti fatigué ?

L'enfance de Munkácsy avait été dure, sans être vraiment une vie d'apprenti menuisier. Peut-être en avait-il subi plus profondément les souffrances, étant né dans un milieu instruit. C'était par ailleurs un avantage, car d'autres apprentis menuisiers n'avaient pas vu dans leur famille de gravures accrochées au mur, et leur carrière d'artiste n'avait pas été favorisée par la famille après quelques premières tentatives. S'il n'avait pas eu un avocat pour tuteur, il n'aurait sûrement pas pu partir comme compagnon d'un peintre ambulant au moment même où, ses certificats en main, il aurait pu augmenter les revenus de la famille... Quelque dur que fût le sort du jeune Munkácsy, il avait été bien soutenu par rapport à ses possibilités : son tuteur lui avait donné un métier, puis une aide matérielle ; le ministre de la culture lui accorda une bourse ; le directeur de la plus grande collection de peintures à Budapest le soutenait moralement ; la presse hongroise lui faisait de la publicité... Il est vrai qu'à Vienne il fut vite congédié de l'Académie, mais ce n'était pas par parti pris contre les Hongrois ; il n'avait simplement pas versé les droits d'étude. A Munich, il ne se sentait pas à l'aise parmi ses compatriotes non plus, mais Ludwig Knaus, le maître de Düsseldorf qu'il avait choisi comme exemple à suivre, lui fit bon accueil, et le Salon de Paris attribua une des médailles d'or à son tableau *le Dernier Jour d'un condamné*, qui détermina en gros les futures conceptions artistiques de Munkácsy.

Peut-être aurait-il été préférable pour lui d'obtenir ce succès plus tard, après avoir mieux assimilé à Munich ou ailleurs ce « métier » de peintre que les impressionnistes, virtuoses de l'art, avaient appris à l'Académie Julian et les post-impressionnistes auprès des précédents. Munkácsy n'avait fait que commencer cette école, sans l'achever, à cause de ses succès précoces. A notre avis, c'était en partie la raison de ce manque de confiance en soi qui l'accompagna pendant toute sa vie, et qu'on discerne aussi bien dans l'expression effacée de l'autoportrait de sa fresque tardive qu'au début des années 1870 quand, à l'apogée de sa popularité, il ru-

newspaper accounts of the balls and receptions at his palace in Paris. In contrast the face of his self-portrait in the Art History Museum in Vienna seems somehow frightened. It was painted among many great artists to proclaim the apotheosis of the Renaissance on a huge ceiling panneau. "A portrayal verging on self-irony" is what we can read in his primary monograph. Is it self-irony or an instinctive confession? The fear of a possible failure is undoubtedly hidden in it. Throughout his life, Munkácsy seems to have been haunted by a tormenting thought: what would happen if his fame—in winning the gold medal of the Salon at the age of 26—with all its attendant money and prestige, suddenly turned out to be a dream—the dream of a tired child apprentice?

Munkácsy's apprenticeship was not a happy one. In the same instance it was not a typical carpenter's apprenticeship because he had certain advantages over the other boys. Firstly, in the homes of the other apprentices, there were no engravings. Secondly, his adopted family supported his early artistic endeavours. Even though he came from an intellectual background he understood well the sufferings of the apprentice life. Without a lawyer for a guardian Munkácsy could hardly have started on his journey as the apprentice to an itinerant painter; especially at a time, when, with a journeyman's certificate in his hand, he could have contributed to his adopted family's income. Despite the hardships of his youth, Munkácsy's career started off well. His guardian helped him in his chosen vocation and later on gave him financial support. The Minister of Culture awarded him a scholarship, the director of the largest painting collection in Pest gave him moral encouragement, while the newly emerging Hungarian press gave him publicity. Sure, in Vienna, because he did not pay the tuition fee, he was soon sent away from the Academy. Although he tried to find his place in Munich, where some of his fellow countrymen worked, he was unsuccessful. The Düsseldorf master, Ludwig Knaus, whom Munkácsy chose as his example, welcomed him. The Paris Salon awarded *The Condemned Cell* a "médaille d'or". This was the picture that would later determine Munkácsy's artistic conception.

In retrospect perhaps it would have been better if this success had come later, after he had had time to consolidate and cultivate his professional training in Munich or elsewhere. The Impressionists gained some of their expertise in the Julian Academy. The post-Impressionists learned from them. Munkácsy started this school but perhaps because of his abrupt success he terminated his involvement with them. The lack of a professional "certificate" probably explained his lack of self-confidence which marked his whole life. It can be detected in the frightened expression of his self-portrait on the ceiling panneau in Vienna.

zu denken, daß Rippl-Rónai am Anfang seiner Laufbahn einer der Gehilfen Munkácsys in Paris war und an seiner Seite sich all das aneignen konnte, dem er später den Rücken kehrte. Munkácsy dagegen hatte keinen richtungsweisenden Meister und, was sehr wichtig ist, nicht einmal eine ordentlich vollendete Ausbildung an der Münchner Akademie hinter sich! Er war in diesem Sinne wirklich ein selfmade-man: ein Märchenheld der Gründerzeit. Die anderen, die nach ihm kamen, hatten zumindest einen Munkácsy als Lehrmeister; ihn selbst brachte ein unbedeutender Maler der ungarischen Provinz, Elek Szamossy, auf den Weg.

Wie Munkácsy selbst über seine Erfolge dachte, ist eine andere Frage. Sicherlich freute er sich über sie, genoß die Zeitungsnotizen, die über die Empfänge und Bälle in seinem Pariser Palais berichteten. Wer aber das gewaltige Gemälde Munkácsys im Wiener Kunsthistorischen Museum, eine Apotheose der Renaissance, betrachtet, findet in der Gruppe der großen Künstler ein Selbstbildnis des Meisters, wie er erschrocken um sich blickt. „Eine beinahe schon die Grenze der Selbstverhöhnung streifende Darstellung", heißt es in der grundlegenden Munkácsy-Monographie. Wäre es wirklich Selbstverspottung? Oder ein unwillkürliches Eingeständnis? Jedenfalls steckt darin eine gewisse Angst vor der möglichen Blamage. Munkácsy verbrachte sein ganzes Leben in einem gewissen Streßzustand: Was wird, wenn er eines schönen Morgens erkennen muß, daß die dem Sechsundzwanzigjährigen verliehene Goldmedaille des Salons und all der Ruhm und all das Geld, was ihm hinterher in den Schoß fiel, bloß der Traum eines müden Lehrlings war?

Munkácsys Kindheit war trübe, aber doch kein typisches Tischlerlehrlingsschicksal. Vielleicht erlebte er die Leiden des Lehrlings gerade darum so intensiv, weil er eigentlich in einer zur Intelligenz gehörenden Familie geboren worden war. Sicher hatte das auch Vorteile für ihn, denn bei den Verwandten anderer Tischlerlehrlinge hingen keine Stiche an den Wänden. Verwaisten Tischlergesellen pflegten die Verwandten keine Künstlerlaufbahn aufgrund von primitiven Zeichnungen, ersten Versuchen zu ebnen. Wer nicht einen Intellektuellen zum Vormund hatte, der hätte mit dem Gesellenbrief in der Tasche kaum den Weg als Gehilfe eines Wandermalers antreten können, sondern wäre wahrscheinlich zum Geldverdienen durch das Handwerk gezwungen worden... Ein schweres Schicksal hatte der junge Munkácsy zweifellos, aber in Anbetracht seiner Möglichkeiten genoß er doch manchen Vorteil. Sein Vormund ließ ihn ein ehrbares Handwerk erlernen und unterstützte ihn auch später. Das Kultusministerium gewährte ihm ein Stipendium, der Leiter der größten Pester Gemäldesammlung moralische Unterstützung und die zu Ansehen gelangte ungarische Presse machte

minait des projets de suicide. La sécurité matérielle assurée par un contrat de dix ans avec son marchand de tableaux, et les louanges chantées en chœur par la presse bien organisée pouvaient assoupir pour un temps ce sentiment, mais il se trouva immédiatement ravivé lorsque, les dix ans écoulés, le marchand n'avait pas renouvelé le contrat avantageux et que, lors de l'exécution du panneau de plafond de Vienne, Munkácsy n'avait pu utiliser ses moyens habituels.

Il en possédait plusieurs. L'un, c'était un très grand nombre d'études, un travail long et pénible pour construire la composition. Une partie des études n'étaient pas des dessins : il lui arrivait, pour peindre les grandes scènes de masse, d'habiller ses modèles, de les disposer selon une esquisse, puis de les photographier. A cet arrangement scénique s'ajoutait une perspective qui manquait de hardiesse. L'unité des scènes historiques ou de genre était assurée par une composition relevant du biedermeier, qu'il avait apprise chez Ludwig Knaus : il y a toujours un personnage, central que regardent les autres. C'est ce qui caractérise le *Dernier Jour d'un condamné*, les *Faiseuses de charpie*, le *Calvaire*, la *Conquête de la Hongrie*, la *Grève* et *Ecce homo*... *Le Christ au prétoire* est devenu le meilleur des tableaux à plusieurs personnages parce qu'ici le tableau a comme deux centres. Et ajoutons encore que le contraste entre les deux personnages qui se font face n'est pas dû à des références « littéraires » aux connaissances des spectateurs sur les Évangiles, mais à des moyens purement picturaux. Les taches claires des vêtements du Christ et de Pilate — l'un allongé à la manière gothique, comme un point d'exclamation, l'autre presque dilué — expriment à elles seules la lutte de deux systèmes mondiaux et annoncent celui qui en sortira victorieux.

L'ordonnance théâtrale et l'angle visuel habituel n'étaient pas applicables à la fresque de Vienne. Munkácsy avait été obligé de demander le concours de peintres plus versés en perspective. Et il n'avait pu user que dans une mesure réduite de son « instrument de travail » le plus important, le fond de bitume brun et noir, dont on ne savait pas encore qu'une fois oxydé, il noircissait peu à peu les peintures. Malheureusement, Munkácsy ne renonça pas tout à fait à ce procédé répandu en Allemagne, même quand on eut déjà découvert cette propriété dangereuse du bitume. C'est que le fond sombre créait à lui seul une certaine harmonie entre les vives couleurs qu'aimait notre artiste. Ses harmonies de couleurs sont certes loin de l'orchestration de tons des impressionnistes, puis de celle, tour à tour assourdie et éclatante, d'un Van Gogh, d'un Gauguin et d'un Cézanne, mais les tableaux de Munkácsy produisent quand même des harmonies simples et saisissantes, des mélodies pures en brun, en vert et en rouge.

Les périodes de son art ont été fort différentes les unes des autres. Dans quelle période

Financial security given by a ten-year contract with his art dealer and the acclaim of a well organized press could do little to allay his fears. But when his art dealer refused to renew this advantageous contract his suppressed fears rose to the surface. In the early 1870s, at the height of his popularity he attempted to commit suicide. When he was working on the ceiling panneau in Vienna Munkácsy could not employ his usual methods. He had several methods. One of them involved making a great number of drawings which contributed to the final study. It was often slow and exacting work. Another of his methods included costume photography. In some of the large crowd scenes, for example, his models were dressed, posed and photographed from a basic compositional sketch, in a simple perspective.

In his historical and genre paintings Munkácsy learned to attain a stage-like compositional unity which was a structural characteristic of the Biedermeier period. He borrowed this from Ludwig Knaus. There is a central figure watched by others. The viewers in the end are themselves viewed! This characterizes *The Condemned Cell*, *Lint Makers*, *Golgotha*, *Árpád's Conquest of Hungary*, and *Ecce Homo*. In *Christ Before Pilate* he evaded this scheme by creating two focal centres in the picture. This lifelike painting is the best of Munkácsy's *tableaux vivants*: Munkácsy showed the conflict between the two central figures by purely artistic means, no reliance being placed upon the viewers' religious convictions. This technique is well exemplified by comparing the white patches on the figures of Christ and Pilate. One of them is distorted like an exclamation mark, stretched almost like a gothic arch. Its companion, in contrast, almost melts away. In this symbolism it is easy to see the large struggle between the two world systems of temporal and religious power and perhaps even the victor of that struggle. Munkácsy had to ask for help from painters more experienced in perspective when engaged on his Viennese commission. Both his techniques of theatrical arrangement and simple perspective alignment could not be used on the ceiling fresco in Vienna. He was unable, moreover, to use extensively his preferred foundation of brownish-black asphalt which typified so many of his paintings. Although it was subsequently discovered that the oxidation of bitumen in the asphalt foundation darkens pictures, he unfortunately still continued to use this method, which was popular in Germany at that time. He liked to use this dark foundation probably because it emphasized the bright colours, that he preferred. He orchestrated his browns, greens, and reds into a clear, captivating harmony.

It is difficult to decide which are Munkácsy's finest pictures because his various periods of artistic creation contrast strongly from each other. Indeed, it is difficult to know which

für ihn Reklame... In Wien wurde er allerdings von der Akademie relegiert, aber nicht etwa wegen eines ungarnfeindlichen Vorurteils, sondern weil er das Lehrgeld nicht zahlte. Er fand seinen Platz auch nicht in München unter den dort studierenden Landsleuten, doch der Düsseldorfer Meister Ludwig Knaus, den er sich zum Vorbild gewählt hatte, nahm ihn freundlich auf, und der Pariser Salon prämierte sein Werk „Der letzte Tag eines Verurteilten" mit der „Médaille d'or": Dies war das Gemälde, das eigentlich die spätere malerische Auffassung Munkácsys in nicht geringem Maße vorausbestimmte.

Es wäre vielleicht besser gewesen, wenn der Erfolg erst später gekommen wäre, wenn er in München oder sonstwo das Malerhandwerk bis zu der Vollkommenheit erlernt hätte, wie es die Impressionisten auf der Julian-Akademie und die Nachimpressionisten von den Impressionisten erlernten. Munkácsy hat die Schulen nur begonnen, aber - eben wegen des plötzlichen Erfolges - nicht beendet. Unserer Meinung nach lag es daran, daß er sein ganzes Leben unter einem Mangel an Selbstvertrauen litt. Zu erkennen ist das sowohl an der angstvollen Geste des Selbstbildnisses auf dem erwähnten Wiener Deckengemälde wie daran, daß er sich zu Beginn der 70er Jahre, auf dem Gipfel seiner frühen Erfolge, mit Selbstmordgedanken trug. Ein mit seinem Kunsthändler auf zehn Jahre geschlossener Vertrag und die Lobeshymnen der ihm wohlgesinnten Presse konnten ihm das Gefühl der Sicherheit geben und die düsteren Gedanken vertreiben, die aber gleich wieder zurückkehrten, als dieser Kunsthändler den vorteilhaften Vertrag nicht erneuerte und Munkácsy bei der Ausführung des Wiener Gemäldes sich nicht auf seine gewohnten „Hilfsmittel" stützen konnte.

Er bediente sich nämlich verschiedener Hilfsmittel. Zu seinen Vorstudien, dem langsamen, fast qualvollen Aufbau seiner Gemälde gehörte zum Beispiel, daß er bei den großen Massenszenen seine Modelle aufgrund einer Kompositionsskizze in Kostüme steckte, posieren ließ und fotografierte. Zu diesen bühnenmäßig eingestellten Gruppen gesellte sich eine peinlich genaue Atelierperspektive. Die Einheitlichkeit seiner historischen oder Genreszenen sicherte Munkácsy nach einem bewährten, noch im Biedermeier verwurzelten Schema, das er Ludwig Knaus abgeguckt hatte: Es ist immer eine zentrale Figur da, und die anderen sehen diese an. So zum Beispiel auf den Gemälden „Der letzte Tag eines Verurteilten", „Scharpiezupferinnen", „Kreuzigung", „Landnahme", „Streik" und „Ecce Homo"; nur bei dem Werk „Christus vor Pilatus" vermied er diese Schablone und konnte eben dadurch mehr Leben in die vielfigurige Komposition bringen, da dieses Bild zwei Schwerpunkte hat. So wurde es zur besten der großen Tafeln. Hinzuzufügen ist, daß Munkácsy den Gegensatz zwischen den zwei einander gegenüberstehen-

reconnaître le « vrai Munkácsy » ? Un esthète hongrois, connu pour la finesse de ses observations, l'a découvert dans l'auteur des esquisses et des études, en évitant la vulgarisation exempte de toute analyse qui se bornait à admirer sans réserve tout l'œuvre du célèbre peintre, mais aussi les jugements trop sévères sur son éloignement des courants modernes. Il est indiscutable que le talent du peintre se manifeste le plus fidèlement dans les esquisses faites comme travail d'atelier, ainsi que dans les études que n'influençait pas le goût des clients bourgeois. Cependant, on ne peut pas négliger non plus les œuvres que les historiens hongrois de l'art considèrent comme les produits du « réalisme romantique » et dont le caractère spécifiquement hongrois fut plus d'une fois mis en relief par les chercheurs traitant l'œuvre de Munkácsy. Ils le faisaient cependant en accordant parfois peu d'attention au langage pictural, à côté des valeurs de la conception morale et de la vision du monde qui s'y manifestent. Aux environs de 1950, Munkácsy devint pour les artistes hongrois un modèle à suivre selon les « prescriptions officielles » ; ce talent original, jadis indépendant des académies, se transforma en schéma académique. Par réaction, l'art de Munkácsy perdit considérablement de sa popularité. Pourtant, les paysages précoces de Barbizon aux chaudes couleurs verdâtres et brunâtres, les scènes de genre des années 1870, les *vedute* des années 1880, inondées de lumière, ainsi que certains magnifiques portraits ou études de portraits sont de réelles réussites. Bornons-nous aux plus importants : *le Condamné*, (dont l'éclairage à la bougie a été inventé par un dur Goya de la *puszta* — pour citer le célèbre historien de l'art Julius Meier-Graefe qui, par ailleurs, tenait Munkácsy pour un simple disciple de W. Leibl) ; les *Adieux* ; le *Mont de Piété* d'une conception fort intéressante, conservé à New York ; *la Femme aux fagots* ; *A l'atelier* ; *Milton* ; *Intérieur parisien* ; les portraits de *Paál* et de *Haynald* ; les versions du *Chemin poussiéreux* ; les champs et allées peints à Jouy-en-Josas, à La Malou et à Colpach... En l'espace de trente ans seulement, Munkácsy a produit six cents tableaux, en partie d'immenses toiles, à un rythme forcé, par rapport à ses contemporains et malgré sa fortune, dans des conditions qui ne favorisaient point le travail créateur.

Son œuvre n'est toujours pas intégralement connu. Il est à supposer que des douzaines de ses tableaux inconnus se trouvent encore dispersés à travers le monde, dans des musées de moindre importance et des collections particulières. Le goût de nos jours a relégué à l'arrière-plan ses œuvres dans lesquelles, pourtant, la bourgeoisie aisée du dernier quart du XIXᵉ siècle avait trouvé le plus pleinement, pendant longtemps, sa propre expression.

Si nous examinons l'art de Munkácsy sans parti pris et compte tenu des enseignements de

periods best exemplify the artist. An important Hungarian art critic disagreed with both the unqualified admiration surrounding Munkácsy, and with his condemnation and detachment from modern movements. He saw Munkácsy primarily as a painter of sketches and studies. His talent, without doubt, is best reflected in those sketches and studies which are uninfluenced by the demands of his patrons. In the same instance we cannot disregard those of his pictures which are referred to in Hungarian art history as the works of "romantic realism". These have a special Hungarian characteristic and they have often been emphasized by scholars dealing with Munkácsy. While praising the moral concept of a picture they often failed to appreciate the artistic presentation. In 1950, Munkácsy, although independent from academies for most of the time was "officially recognized" as an academic painter. He was stereotyped.

The younger generation of artists and amateurs reacted to this official claim with hostility. His art lost much of its popularity. His pictures were viewed as dusty relics from the past; even though a lively experience, an instinctive talent and a deep humanism can be sensed in them. The warm greenish-brown Barbizonian landscapes, the genre paintings of the seventies and the shining vedutas of the 1880s are real masterpieces. The most important of these are: *The Condemned*, whose "candle-lighting"—according to the renowned art historian Julius Meier-Graefe—"was invented by a tough Goya from the puszta". This was quite a compliment for one who regarded Munkácsy as only a mere follower of the German painter W. Leibl. We can mention *Farewell*; and the very interestingly conceived *The Pawnbroker's Shop* which is in New York; *Woman Carrying Faggots*; *In the Studio*; *Milton*; *Paris Interior*; the portraits of *László Paál* and *Haynald*; the variants of *Dusty Road* and the pictures he painted in Jouy-en-Josas, La Malou and Colpach.

He worked at a frantic pace. In three decades he amassed 600 pictures, some of them huge canvases. Although compared to some of his contemporaries he was well off, he often worked amidst a multitude of unfavourable circumstances which made creative art seem unwelcome.

Even today his life work is not fully known. It is probable that throughout the world there are dozens of unrecorded Munkácsy pictures in small museums and private collections. In the last quarter of the nineteenth century his pictures were sought after by the wealthy. Today his paintings are unfashionable, having been discarded by modern taste.

If we study Munkácsy's art in an objective way, without prejudice and elaborated by our present knowledge, we will discover much. His pictures not only reveal the negative aspects of past artistic contradictions; but in them we

den Personen nicht nur durch Hinweise auf die bei dem Beschauer vorausgesetzten Kenntnisse des Evangeliums, sondern auch durch rein malerische Mittel erreichte: durch die Verschiedenheit der hellen Flächen der Kleider von Christus und Pilatus. Die eine ist wie ein gotisch langgestrecktes Ausrufungszeichen, die andere weich, amöbenartig zerfließend. Dies allein drückt den Kampf zweier Welten aus und läßt den Sieger erkennen.

Diese theatralische Anordnung und der gewohnte Gesichtswinkel waren aber auf dem Deckengemälde nicht mehr anwendbar. Munkácsy war in Wien genötigt, die Hilfe zweier in der Perspektive gewandteren Maler in Anspruch zu nehmen. Auch das für ihn wichtigste Hilfsmittel, die bräunlichschwarze Asphaltgrundierung, konnte er da nur in geringem Maße in Anspruch nehmen. Damals wußte man noch nicht, daß der allmählich oxydierende Asphaltgrund das Bild unaufhaltsam verdunkelt. Er gab aber dieses in Deutschland weit verbreitete Verfahren leider auch dann nicht auf, als die gefährlichen Eigenschaften des Bitumens bereits bekannt geworden waren. Der dunkle Grund vermochte nämlich eine gewisse Harmonie der von Munkácsy bevorzugten lebhaften Farben gewährleisten. Diese Harmonie steht zwar weit hinter dem Orchester zurück, das die Farben der Impressionisten, sodann Van Goghs, Gauguins und Cézannes in allen Tönen und Lautstärken erklingen ließ, dafür aber ertönen auf den besten Munkácsy-Bildern die braunen, grünen und roten Farben wie eine einfache, lichte, ergreifende Melodie.

In der Kunst Munkácsys bestehen ziemlich starke Unterschiede zwischen den einzelnen Perioden. Aus welcher lernen wir den „echten" Munkácsy kennen? Ein ungarischer Ästhetiker mit feinem Empfinden meinte, es sei der Maler der Skizzen und Studien, wodurch er von der das gesamte Werk des erfolgreichen Künstlers kritiklos bewundernden Popularisierung abrückte, aber auch von dem strengen Urteil, das wegen der Distanzierung von den modernen Bewegungen ausgesprochen wurde. Zweifellos lassen am besten die als Werkstattarbeit hingeworfenen frischen Skizzen, die noch nicht unter dem Geschmacksterror der großbürgerlichen Auftraggeber litten, das Talent des Malers erkennen. Aber man sollte auch jene Bilder nicht außer Acht lassen, die in der ungarischen Kunstgeschichte gewöhnlich als Schöpfungen eines „romantischen Realismus" bezeichnet werden und deren spezifisch nationale Züge die sich mit Munkácsy befassenden Wissenschaftler wiederholt hervorhoben. Sie taten es allerdings oft so, daß sie neben den moralischen und weltanschaulichen Werten dieser Bilder nur ein geringes Gewicht auf das Malerische legten. So konnte Munkácsy um 1950 das „offiziell empfohlene" Vorbild werden: Das von den einstigen Akademien unabhängige originelle Talent sollte nun akademische Schablone sein.

l'évolution ultérieure, nous constaterons que cette peinture ne s'attachait pas exclusivement à un seul courant, peu apprécié aujourd'hui, de son époque. Nous y découvrirons aussi la légèreté, avide des miracles de ce monde, des impressionnistes, ainsi que la grandeur morale opiniâtre, assumant la responsabilité pour le monde entier, des post-impressionnistes.

can also see both the ease of the Impressionist and the moral greatness of the post-Impressionist.

Angesichts dieser offiziellen Verherrlichung verlor Munkácsy in den Augen der jungen Künstler- und Liebhabergeneration viel von seinem Prestige. Jedoch sind viele der warmen, grünlich-bräunlichen Barbizoner Landschaften, der Genrebilder der siebziger Jahre, der leuchtenden Stilleben der achtziger Jahre und einige Porträts oder Kopfstudien meisterhaft gelungene Werke, die jeder noch so strengen Kritik standhalten. Zu erwähnen sind hier seine wichtigsten Bilder: „Der Verurteilte" (von dessen Kerzenlicht selbst Julius Meier-Graefe, der übrigens in Munkácsy einfach einen der Leibl-Nachfolger sah, meinte: „Der ... hat das Visionäre Rembrandts und ist von einem starkknöchigen Goya der Puśta erfunden); „Abschied"; das in New York verwahrte, in der Auffassung sehr interessante „Leihhaus"; die „Reisigtragende Frau"; „Im Atelier"; „Milton"; das „Pariser Interieur"; die Porträts des Malers László Paál und des Erzbischofs Haynald; die Varianten von „Staubiger Weg" und nicht zuletzt die in Jouy-en-Josas, La Malou und in Colpach gemalten Wiesen und Alleen.

Munkácsy malte ungefähr 600 Bilder, zum Teil sogar Riesengemälde, im ganzen in drei Jahrzehnten, in gehetztem Tempo und trotz allem Wohlstand unter für die schöpferische Arbeit ungünstigen Umständen. Die heutige Kunstwissenschaft kennt Munkácsys Lebenswerk noch immer nicht ausreichend. Es ist sehr wahrscheinlich, daß sich in den kleineren Museen und Privatsammlungen der Welt Dutzende von unbekannten Munkácsy-Bildern verstecken. Der heutige Geschmack findet wenig Freude an den „Salonbildern". Aber man sollte nicht vergessen, daß es eben diese Bilder sein dürften, in denen der wohlhabende Bürger im letzten Viertel des vorigen Jahrhunderts die volle Verwirklichung seines Wesens erkannte.

Wenn wir, belehrt durch die spätere Entwicklung, aber doch unbefangen, Munkácsys Kunst beurteilen, müssen wir erkennen, daß seine Malerei keineswegs einer einzigen, heute weniger geschätzten Geschmacksrichtung verpflichtet war. Vielmehr können wir in seinen Bildern sowohl die leichte, die Wunder der Welt verschlingende Kunst der Impressionisten, aber auch die moralische Größe der zähen, die Verantwortung für die Welt erkennenden Nachimpressionisten entdecken.

Données biographiques

1844 — Il naît à Munkács (actuellement Mukatchevo — Union Soviétique) le 20 février. Son père, Leó Mihály Lieb, d'une famille d'origine bavaroise, est fonctionnaire. Jusqu'à l'âge de vingt-deux ans, l'artiste figure dans les documents officiels sous le nom de Mihály Lieb.

1851 — Les deux parents étant morts, les enfants sont pris en charge par les oncles et les tantes. Le tuteur de Munkácsy est l'avocat István Reök, qui ne peut exercer sa profession à cause du rôle qu'il a joué pendant la guerre d'Indépendance.

1854-58 — Munkácsy apprend le métier de menuisier, mais c'est surtout le dessin et la peinture qui l'intéressent. Il fait la connaissance du peintre Elek Szamossy, qui a étudié à l'Académie des Arts de Vienne, auprès de Rahl.

1861-62 — Il parcourt le pays comme élève de Szamossy, fait des restaurations, peint des portraits.

1863-64 — Il se rend à Pest et se rallie à la vie artistique qui commence à se développer dans la ville. Il fait la connaissance du peintre Antal Ligeti qui l'aide avec dévouement. Il peint des scènes de genre populaires.

1865 — Il fait des études à Vienne, à l'Académie, comme élève de Rahl.

1866 — Il se rend à Munich où travaillent à l'époque la plupart des peintres hongrois.

1867 — Il obtient une bourse de József Eötvös, ministre de la Culture du nouveau gouvernement hongrois. Il visite l'exposition universelle de Paris, où il voit pour la première fois les œuvres de Courbet.

1868 — De Munich, il va à Düsseldorf afin d'étudier auprès de son idéal, Ludwig Knaus, auteur de scènes de genre. Knaus l'accueille cordialement, l'aide à faire carrière. L'œuvre la plus réussie de ces débuts est l'*Aurore*, actuellement perdue (*Apprenti bâillant*).

1870 — Sa composition à plusieurs personnages, *le Dernier Jour d'un condamné*, obtient, de façon inattendue, la médaille d'or du Salon de Paris.

1871 — *Faiseuses de charpie* lui apporte un nouveau succès. Il s'établit à Paris. Parmi ses amis intimes, on trouve le paysagiste hongrois László Paál qui travaille à Barbizon, et un aristocrate amateur d'arts, le baron de Marches.

1872-73 — Munkácsy travaille à Colpach (Luxembourg), dans le domaine de De Marches. Après son succès inattendu, il fait une dépression. A la mort du baron, il épouse sa veuve et s'installe à Paris. Il se rend souvent à Barbizon, pour travailler, c'est la période où il peint les meilleurs paysages de sa carrière. A l'exposition universelle de Vienne, en 1873, il a un grand succès

Biographical Notes

1844 — Munkácsy was born on February 20, in Munkács (now Mukatchevo, USSR). His father, Leó Mihály Lieb, of Bavarian descent, was a civil servant. Up to the age of twenty-two the painter appears as Mihály Lieb in official documents.

1851 — After the death of both parents, the children are taken in by uncles and aunts. Munkácsy's guardian is István Reök, a lawyer who is forced to give up his practice because of the role he played in the 1848/49 War of Independence.

1854-58 — Munkácsy learns the joiner's trade, but he is more interested in drawing and painting. He meets Elek Szamossy, a painter who studied at the Academy in Vienna as the pupil of Rahl.

1861-62 — Munkácsy travels all over the country as Szamossy's pupil; he restores pictures and paints portraits.

1863-64 — He goes to Pest, and joins the slowly emerging art life of the town. He meets Antal Ligeti, a painter who altruistically encourages his endeavours. Munkácsy paints popular genre pictures.

1865 — Continues his studies at the Academy in Vienna as Rahl's pupil.

1866 — Goes to Munich, where the majority of Hungarian painters work at this time.

1867 — He is awarded a scholarship by Baron József Eötvös, the Minister of Culture of the new Hungarian Government. He visits the world exhibition in Paris, where he sees Courbet's works for the first time.

1868 — From Munich he goes to Düsseldorf to learn from his idol, Ludwig Knaus, the genre painter. Knaus welcomes Munkácsy and smooths the path for his career. His most successful work from this period is the lost *Yawning Apprentice*.

1870 — *The Condemned Cell*, a composition with many figures, unexpectedly wins a gold medal at the exhibition of the Paris Salon.

1871 — Another success is *Lint Makers*. Munkácsy moves to Paris: staying there at the time are his friends László Paál, the Hungarian painter working in Barbizon, and Baron de Marches, the art patron aristocrat.

1872-73 — Munkácsy works at Colpach, Luxembourg on the De Marches estate. After his sudden and swift success, Munkácsy is overcome by depression. When the baron dies, Munkácsy marries his widow and settles in Paris. He goes to Barbizon frequently to paint; this period produces the best of his landscape painting. His popular genre pictures achieve great success at the 1873 world exhibition in Vienna (*Tramps of the Night, Woman Churning*). "Munkácsy is one of the most determined and most unrestrained realists of Europe", writes V. V. Stasov, the

Biographische Angaben

1844. 20. Februar – Geboren in Munkács (heute Mukatschevo, UdSSR). Der Vater Leó Mihály Lieb war Staatsbeamter bayrischen Ursprungs. Der Maler wurde bis zu seinem zweiundzwanzigsten Lebensjahr als Mihály Lieb in den amtlichen Papieren geführt.

1851 – Nach dem Tod beider Eltern nehmen die Geschwister der Eltern die verwaisten Kinder zu sich. Vormund des Knaben wird der Rechtsanwalt István Reök, der wegen seiner Teilnahme an dem Freiheitskrieg von 1848–49 Berufsverbot erhielt.

1854-58 – Der junge Munkácsy erlernt das Tischlerhandwerk, interessiert sich jedoch immer mehr für das Zeichnen und Malen. Bekanntschaft mit dem Kunstmaler Elek Szamossy, der früher an der Wiener Akademie Rahls Malklasse besuchte.

1861/62 – Als Schüler·Szamossys zieht er mit seinem Meister durch das Land, restauriert Bilder und malt Porträts.

1863/64 – Erstmalig in Pest, wo sich der angehende Maler in das bescheidene Kunstleben der Stadt einschaltet. Bekanntschaft mit dem Maler Antal Ligeti, der den Anfänger selbstlos unterstützt. Munkácsy malt volkstümliche Genrebilder.

1865 – Fortsetzung der Studien in Wien an der Akademie bei Rahl.

1866 – Übersiedlung nach München, wo um diese Zeit die meisten ungarischen Maler arbeiten.

1867 – Die neue Regierung erkennt ihm ein Stipendium zu. Besuch der Pariser Weltausstellung, hier begegnet er zum erstenmal den Werken Courbets.

1868 – Fortsetzung der Studien in Düsseldorf, um seinem Vorbild, dem Genremaler Ludwig Knaus, nahe zu sein. Knaus nimmt den jungen Maler gütig auf und ebnet seinen Weg. Das beste Werk dieser Frühzeit ist „Im Morgengrauen" („Gähnender Lehrling", verschollen).

1870 – „Der letzte Tag eines Verurteilten", die vielfigurige Komposition, gewinnt überraschenderweise auf der Ausstellung im Pariser Salon eine der Goldmedaillen.

1871 – Neuerlichen Erfolg bringt ihm das Gemälde „Scharpiezupferinnen" ein. Munkácsy verlegt seinen Wohnsitz nach Paris. Zu seinen nächsten Freunden gehörten der in Barbizon tätige ungarische Landschaftsmaler László Paál und der Kunstliebhaber Baron de Marches.

1872-73 – Munkácsy arbeitet in Colpach, Luxemburg, auf dem Gut des Barons de Marches. Nach dem unerwartet raschen Erfolg bemächtigt sich seiner eine Depression. Als der Baron stirbt, hält Munkácsy um die Hand der Witwe an und läßt sich in Paris nieder. Viel Zeit verbringt er in Barbizon, wo

avec ses scènes de genre populaires *(Vagabonds de nuit, la Femme à la baratte)*. « Munkácsy est un des réalistes les plus résolus, les plus effrénés d'Europe » — écrit V. V. Stassov, idéologue russe des « pérédvijnik » (mouvement russe de peinture).

1874 — Il se rend en Hongrie avec sa femme. Comme souvenir de ce voyage, il peint des paysages hongrois *(Chemin poussiéreux)*. Il crée son meilleur tableau de salon *A l'atelier*. Il s'éloigne du genre des scènes réalistes de la vie du peuple.

1877 — Pour 30 000 francs, il vend son tableau *Milton* à son nouveau marchand de tableaux, Charles Sedelmeyer. Il mène un train de vie élégant à Paris.

1878 — Le train de vie coûteux astreint Munkácsy à conclure avec Sedelmeyer un contrat pour une durée de dix ans, avantageux du point de vue matériel, mais d'une influence défavorable sur l'évolution de l'artiste. Par la suite, les thèmes et le style des œuvres de Munkácsy seront déterminés par la demande des commerçants et par celle du public aisé.

1881 — C'est la période où Munkácsy exécute ses grandioses compositions à sujet biblique : *le Christ au prétoire*, puis

1884 — *le Calvaire* (tous les deux se trouvent à Philadelphie). La puissance de son talent se manifeste moins dans ces grandes entreprises que dans ses études de paysages et ses portraits moins ambitieux *(Portrait de Lajos Haynald)*. Ses paysages sont en général peints à l'atelier, il y suit les traditions de plein-air de Barbizon. Il se désolidarise par contre nettement de l'impressionnisme. Son état de santé s'aggrave et, à cause de ses douleurs à la colonne vertébrale, il doit faire des cures dans des villes d'eau. Il peint beaucoup de « tableaux de salon », scènes empruntées à la vie de la grande bourgeoisie.

1886 — Son tableau *la Mort de Mozart* n'a plus de succès auprès du public, son style commence à être démodé. Après la mort de l'illustre Makart, le gouvernement de Vienne le charge d'exécuter un des panneaux de plafond, de 100 m², du Kunsthistorisches Museum.

1888 — Il travaille à ce panneau. Dans son atelier, il est aidé par plusieurs peintres dont József Rippl-Rónai. Sedelmeyer ne cesse de vendre ses œuvres, sans renouveler le contrat.

1889 — Le gouvernement hongrois l'invite à peindre la scène symbolique de *la Conquête de la Hongrie* pour l'édifice du Parlement en construction à Budapest.

1890 — Le panneau de plafond de Vienne, *l'Apothéose de la Renaissance*, est achevé.

1891–93 — Il travaille à *la Conquête de la Hongrie*, il prépare plusieurs études de couleur de grandes dimensions. L'œuvre définitive mesure plus de 60 m² et se compose de près de cent figures. L'état de santé de Munkácsy se détériore, des maux de tête incessants le torturent, son niveau intellectuel baisse.

Russian ideologist of the "peredvizhniks".

1874 — He visits Hungary with his wife, and paints his Hungarian landscapes on the basis of memories from his journey *(Dusty Road)*. *The Pawnbroker's Shop* is exhibited at the Salon.

1876 — From this year onwards Munkácsy becomes one of the most popular painters of rich Parisians. He paints his most beautiful drawing-room picture, *In the Studio*—drifting away from the genre of the popular and realistic *tableau vivant*.

1877 — Munkácsy sells *Milton* for thirty thousand franks to his new art dealer, Charles Sedelmeyer. The Munkácsys lead a life of luxury in Paris.

1878 — Their expensive life-style forces the painter to sign a ten-year contract with Sedelmeyer. The contract is financially advantageous, but has an advers influence on his artistic development. From now on, the theme and style of Munkácsy's pictures are determined by the taste of the rich buyers it served.

1881 — Munkácsy works on the great Biblical composition, the huge *Christ before Pilate*, which is followed

1884 — by *Golgotha* (both were taken to Philadelphia). Munkácsy is at his best not in his large compositions, but in his small landscape studies and portraits (e.g. *Portrait of Lajos Haynald*). Most of his landscapes are painted in the studio, but they continue the Barbizonean traditions of plein air painting. However, he decidedly rejects Impressionism. His health gradually deteriorates and his spine complaints force him to seek cure at spa resorts. He paints several drawing-room pictures depicting scenes from the life of the rich bourgeoisie.

1886 — *The Death of Mozart* fails to win the public; his style starts to become outdated. After the death of Makart, the Viennese Government commissions Munkácsy to paint one of the one hundred square metres ceiling panneaus of the Kunsthistorisches Museum.

1888 — He works on the ceiling panneau. He employs several apprentices in his studio, among them József Rippl-Rónai. Sedelmeyer continues to sell his works, but does not renew the profitable contract.

1889 — The Hungarian Government commissions Munkácsy to paint the symbolic scene of *Árpád's Conquest of Hungary* for the Parliament then under construction in Budapest.

1890 — The Viennese panneau, *The Apotheosis of the Renaissance*, is completed.

1891–93 — He works on *Árpád's Conquest of Hungary*. Several large colour sketches are made for the picture. The size of the completed work is over sixty square metres, with almost one hundred figures. Munkácsy's health gradually deteriorates, he is tormented by continual headache and his intellect declines rapidly.

er seine schönsten Landschaften malt. Auf der Wiener Weltausstellung 1873 haben seine volkstümlichen Genrebilder („Nächtliche Vagabunden", „Frau beim Buttern") großen Erfolg. „Munkácsy ist einer der entschiedensten und zügellosesten Realisten Europas", schreibt W. W. Stassow, der geistige Führer der russischen „Peredwishniki" (Wanderaussteller).

1874 – Besuch in Ungarn mit seiner Frau. Aufgrund der Reiseerlebnisse malt er ungarische Landschaften („Fahrt auf der Pußta"). – Ausstellung des Gemäldes „Leihhaus" im Pariser Salon.

1876 – Nun gehört Munkácsy zu den beliebtesten Malern der „oberen Zehntausend" in Paris. Er malt das schönste seiner sogenannten Salonbilder, „Im Atelier". Er gibt das Malen von volkstümlichen realistischen Genrebildern auf.

1877 – Sein neuer Kunsthändler Charles Sedelmeyer kauft den „Milton" für dreißigtausend Francs. Der Meister unterhält ein kleines Palais in Paris.

1878 – Die kostspielige Lebensweise nötigt Munkácsy, mit Sedelmeyer einen Vertrag für zehn Jahre abzuschließen. Der Vertrag ist finanziell vorteilhaft, aber für die weitere Entwicklung des Künstlers schädlich. Nun malt er eine ganze Folge von Bildern, deren Themen und Stil der Kunsthandel sowie der Anspruch des vornehmen Publikums, das er bedient, bestimmen.

1881 – Das Jahr der großen biblischen Kompositionen: „Christus vor Pilatus" und später

1884 – „Kreuzigung" (beide in Philadelphia). Die besten malerischen Qualitäten des Meisters äußern sich nicht in den großzügigen Tafeln, sondern in den bescheideneren Landschaften und Porträts („Porträt des Erzbischofs Lajos Haynald"). Die Landschaften malt er meistens im Atelier, hält aber dabei an den Barbizoner Traditionen des Pleinairismus fest. Von den Impressionisten distanziert er sich entschieden. Sein Gesundheitszustand verschlechtert sich, er muß sich wegen Rückenmarkbeschwerden in Kurorten behandeln lassen. Zwischendurch malt er zumeist Salonbilder und Szenen aus dem großbürgerlichen Leben.

1886 – Das Gemälde „Mozarts Tod" wird nicht mehr so günstig aufgenommen, diese Malweise fängt an aus der Mode zu gehen. Die Wiener Regierung beauftragt Munkácsy – nach dem Tod des hochangesehenen Makart–, ein Deckengemälde für das Kunsthistorische Museum auf einer Fläche von hundert Quadratmetern zu malen.

1888 – Arbeit an dem Deckengemälde. Er beschäftigt in seinem Atelier mehrere Gehilfen, unter ihnen József Rippl-Rónai. Sedelmeyer vertreibt Munkácsys Bilder auch weiterhin, will aber den auslaufenden Vertrag nicht erneuern.

1894-96 — Il travaille à ses dernières compositions à plusieurs figures, *la Grève* et *Ecce homo*. Il prend part aux festivités du millénaire de la Hongrie, mais il est déjà gravement malade.

1897-1900 — Peu de temps après ces festivités fatigantes, il doit être soigné dans une maison de santé, puis dans un hôpital psychiatrique. Il passe près de trois ans dans un établissement des environs de Baden-Baden, et devient tout à fait impotent.

1900 — Il meurt le 1er mai à l'hôpital psychiatrique d'Endenich. Ses funérailles somptueuses ont lieu à Budapest. Une partie importante de ses œuvres se trouvant à l'étranger est acquise par des collections hongroises, publiques et particulières, en premier lieu par la Galerie Nationale Hongroise. A Békéscsaba, un musée est consacré à sa mémoire. Ses tableaux, à couche de fond en bitume, qui s'assombrissent lentement mais inévitablement, sont conservés dans des locaux spécialement climatisés. Sa conception du début des années 1870, couleurs étoffées, dramatisme des scènes, a été suivie dans l'entre-deux-guerres par les membres de l'école connue sous le nom de « peintres de la Grande Plaine » — Gyula Rudnay, János Tornyai, Béla Endre et d'autres.

1894-96 — He works on his last many-figured compositions, *Strike* and the large *Ecce Homo*. He participates in the celebrations commemorating the millennium of the Hungarian conquest, but by now he is gravely ill.

1897-1900 — Shortly after the festivities he has to enter a sanatorium, and later has to undergo mental treatment. For almost three years he lives as a helpless invalid in a hospital near Baden-Baden.

1900 — On May 1, he dies at the mental hospital in Endenich. He is buried in Budapest with great pomp. The great majority of his pictures owned by foreigners is acquired by Hungarian public and private collections, mostly by the Hungarian National Gallery. In Békéscsaba, a museum preserves his memory. His bitumen grounded pictures—gradually becoming darker and darker—are kept in rooms fitted with special air conditioners. The art conception of the early 1870s—its full colours and dramatic tension—is followed between the two world wars by a school of painting known as the "Painters of the Great Plain": Gyula Rudnay, János Tornyai, Béla Endre and others.

1889 – Die ungarische Regierung beauftragt Munkácsy, ein symbolisches Gemälde von der Landnahme der Ungarn für das in Budapest zu errichtende Parlament zu malen.

1890 – Beendigung des Deckengemäldes „Apotheose der Renaissance".

1891-93 – Arbeit an der „Landnahme". Es entstehen mehrere großformatige Farbskizzen zum Gemälde. Das fertige Bild ist über sechzig Quadratmeter groß und von nahezu hundert Figuren bevölkert. Der Meister leidet an ständigen Kopfschmerzen und verfällt geistig.

1894-96 – Arbeit an den letzten vielfigurigen Kompositionen, dem „Streik" und dem großformatigen „Ecce Homo". Trotz seines bedenklichen Gesundheitszustandes Teilnahme an den Millenniumsfeierlichkeiten in Budapest.

1897-1900 – Bald nach den anstrengenden Feierlichkeiten wird er von den Ärzten zunächst in ein Sanatorium, dann in eine Nervenheilanstalt eingewiesen. Nahezu drei Jahre verbringt er als unzurechnungsfähiger Kranker in einer Anstalt bei Baden-Baden.

1900 – Stirbt am 1. Mai in Endenich. Begräbnis in Budapest mit großem Pomp. Ein bedeutender Teil seiner Bilder gelangten seitdem von ausländischen Besitzern in ungarische öffentliche und Privatsammlungen, die meisten in die Ungarische Nationalgalerie. In Békéscsaba wurde ein Munkácsy-Museum eingerichtet. Seine auf Bitumengrund gemalten Bilder verdunkeln, sie werden deshalb neuerdings in Räumlichkeiten mit besonderer Klimaanlage verwahrt. Die künstlerische Auffassung, die Munkácsy in den 1870er Jahren volkstümlich machte, mit satten Farben und dramatischen Szenen, wurde von der „Tieflandschule" genannten ungarischen Künstlergruppe aufgegriffen und zwischen den beiden Weltkriegen besonders von den Malern Gyula Rudnay, János Tornyai und Béla Endre fortgesetzt.

Littérature

Munkácsy, Michel de : *Souvenirs. L'enfance.* Paris, 1897
Ilges, W. F. : *Michael von Munkácsy.* Bielefeld-Leipzig, 1899
Sedelmeyer, Charles : *Michael von Munkácsy.* Paris, 1914
Muther, Richard : « Munkácsy ». *Aufsätze* I. Berlin, 1914
Lyka, Karl von : *Michael von Munkácsy.* Vienne, 1926
Pogány, G. : *Mihály Munkácsy.* Dresde, 1954
Végvári, Lajos : « Munkácsys Gemälde : Die Scharpiezupferinnen. » *Acta Historiae Artium*, Budapest, 1955
Végvári, Lajos : *Katalog der Gemälde und Zeichnungen Mihály Munkácsys.* Budapest, 1959
Végvári, Lajos : *Munkácsy.* Budapest, 1961
Perneczky, Géza : *Mihály Munkácsy.* Budapest, 1970 (en anglais)
Székely, András : *Mihály Munkácsy.* Berlin, 1977

Literature

Munkácsy, Michel de: *Souvenirs. L'enfance.* Paris, 1897
Ilges, W. F.: *Michael von Munkácsy.* Bielefeld-Leipzig, 1899
Sedelmeyer, Charles: *Michael von Munkácsy.* Paris, 1914
Muther, Richard: "Munkácsy". *Aufsätze* I. Berlin, 1914
Lyka, Karl von: *Michael von Munkácsy*, Vienna, 1926
Pogány, G.: *Mihály Munkácsy.* Dresden, 1954
Végvári, Lajos: "Munkácsys Gemälde: Die Scharpiezupferinnen." *Acta Historiae Artium*, Budapest, 1955
Végvári, Lajos: *Katalog der Gemälde und Zeichnungen Mihály Munkácsys.* Budapest, 1959
Végvári, Lajos: *Munkácsy.* Budapest, 1961
Perneczky, Géza: *Mihály Munkácsy.* Budapest, 1970 (in English)
Székely, András: *Mihály Munkácsy.* Berlin, 1977

Literatur

Munkácsy, Michel de: *Souvenirs. L'enfance.* Paris 1897 (deutsch: *Erinnerungen. Die Kindheit.* Berlin 1897)
Ilges, F. W.: *Michael von Munkácsy.* Bielefeld-Leipzig 1899
Sedelmeyer, Charles: *Michael von Munkácsy.* Paris 1914
Muther, Richard: „Munkácsy." *Aufsätze* I. Berlin 1914
Lyka, Karl von: *Michael von Munkácsy.* Wien 1926
Pogány, G.: *Mihály Munkácsy.* Dresden 1954
Végvári, Lajos: „Munkácsys Gemälde: Die Scharpiezupferinnen." *Acta Historiae Artium*, Budapest 1955
Végvári, Lajos: *Katalog der Gemälde und Zeichnungen Mihály Munkácsys.* Budapest 1959
Végvári, Lajos: *Munkácsy.* Budapest 1961
Perneczky, Géza: *Mihály Munkácsy.* Budapest 1970 (in englischer Sprache)
Székely, András: *Mihály Munkácsy.* Berlin 1977

17. A la buanderie
   1877. Huile, toile, 46 × 54 cm
   Budapest, Galerie Nationale Hongroise

18. La Rue Sombre
   1871. Huile, bois, 65 × 53 cm
   Budapest, Galerie Nationale Hongroise

19. A la taverne
   Vers 1875. Huile, bois, 32 × 40 cm
   Budapest, Galerie Nationale Hongroise

20. Vagabonds de nuit
   1872/73. Huile, bois, 161,5 × 220 cm
   Budapest, Galerie Nationale Hongroise

21. Vagabonds de nuit (détail)

22. Deux gars attablés (étude pour le tableau
   le Héros du village)
   1874. Huile, toile, 99 × 81 cm
   Békéscsaba, Musée Munkácsy Mihály

23. Le Condamné
   Vers 1872. Huile, bois, 87,5 × 116 cm
   Budapest, Galerie Nationale Hongroise

24. Le Condamné (détail)

25. Esquisse pour le tableau le Mont de Piété
   1871/73. Huile, bois, 91 × 126 cm
   Budapest, Galerie Nationale Hongroise

26. Vieille femme assise (étude pour
   le tableau le Mont de Piété)
   1873/74. Huile, bois, 84 × 64 cm
   Budapest, propriété de Pál Pátzay

27. Mère avec son enfant (étude pour le
   tableau le Mont de Piété)
   1873. Huile, bois, 64,5 × 62 cm
   Budapest, Galerie Nationale Hongroise

28. L'Homme à la cape (étude pour le tableau
   le Mont de Piété)
   1874. Huile, bois, 92 × 72 cm
   Budapest, Galerie Nationale Hongroise

29. Le Mont de Piété
   1874. Huile, toile, 163,5 × 240 cm
   New York, the Metropolitan Museum of Art

30. Le Champ de maïs
   1874. Huile, bois, 67 × 102 cm
   Budapest, Galerie Nationale Hongroise

31. Chemin poussiéreux I
   1874. Huile, bois, 77 × 117,5 cm
   Budapest, Galerie Nationale Hongroise

32. Chemin poussiéreux II
   1874/83. Huile, bois, 96 × 129 cm
   Budapest, Galerie Nationale Hongroise

17. In the Laundry
   1877. Oil on canvas, 46 × 54 cm
   Budapest, Hungarian National Gallery

18. Dark Street
   1871. Oil on wood, 65 × 53 cm
   Budapest, Hungarian National Gallery

19. In the Tavern
   About 1875. Oil on wood, 32 × 40 cm
   Budapest, Hungarian National Gallery

20. Tramps of the Night
   1872/73. Oil on wood, 161,5 × 220 cm
   Budapest, Hungarian National Gallery

21. Tramps of the Night (Detail)

22. Two Youths at the Table (Study for The
   Hero of the Village)
   1874. Oil on canvas, 99 × 81 cm
   Békéscsaba, Munkácsy Mihály Museum

23. The Condemned
   About 1872. Oil on wood, 87.5 × 116 cm
   Budapest, Hungarian National Gallery

24. The Condemned (Detail)

25. Sketch for the Pawnbroker's Shop
   1871/73. Oil on wood, 91 × 126 cm
   Budapest, Hungarian National Gallery

26. Seated Old Woman (Study for The
   Pawnbroker's Shop)
   1873/74. Oil on wood, 84 × 64 cm
   Owned by Pál Pátzay, Budapest

27. Mother and Child (Study for The
   Pawnbroker's Shop)
   1873. Oil on wood, 64.5 × 62 cm
   Budapest, Hungarian National Gallery

28. Man in Coat (Study for The
   Pawnbroker's Shop)
   1874. Oil on wood, 92 × 72 cm
   Budapest, Hungarian National Gallery

29. The Pawnbroker's Shop
   1874. Oil on canvas, 165 × 240 cm
   New York, The Metropolitan Museum of Art

30. The Maize-Field
   1874. Oil on wood, 67 × 102 cm
   Budapest, Hungarian National Gallery

31. Dusty Road I
   1874. Oil on wood, 77 × 117.5 cm
   Budapest, Hungarian National Gallery

32. Dusty Road II
   1874/83. Oil on wood, 96 × 129 cm
   Budapest, Hungarian National Gallery

17. In der Waschküche
   1877. Öl auf Leinwand, 46 × 54 cm
   Budapest, Ungarische Nationalgalerie

18. Dunkle Gasse
   1871. Öl auf Holz, 65 × 53 cm
   Budapest, Ungarische Nationalgalerie

19. In der Schenke
   Um 1875. Öl auf Holz, 32 × 40 cm
   Budapest, Ungarische Nationalgalerie

20. Nächtliche Vagabunden
   1872/73. Öl auf Holz, 161,5 × 220 cm
   Budapest, Ungarische Nationalgalerie

21. Nächtliche Vagabunden (Ausschnitt)

22. Zwei Burschen am Tisch (Studie zu
   Dorffeld)
   1874. Öl auf Leinwand, 99 × 81 cm
   Békéscsaba, Munkácsy-Mihály-Museum

23. Der Verurteilte
   1872. Öl auf Holz, 87,5 × 116 cm
   Budapest, Ungarische Nationalgalerie

24. Der Verurteilte (Ausschnitt)

25. Leihhaus (Skizze)
   1871/73. Öl auf Holz, 91 × 126 cm
   Budapest, Ungarische Nationalgalerie

26. Sitzende alte Frau (Studie zu Leihhaus)
   1873/74. Öl auf Holz, 84 × 64 cm
   Budapest, Im Besitz von Pál Pátzay

27. Mutter mit Kind (Studie zu Leihhaus)
   1873. Öl auf Holz, 64,5 × 62 cm
   Budapest, Ungarische Nationalgalerie

28. Mann mit Mantel (Studie zu Leihhaus)
   1874. Öl auf Holz, 92 × 72 cm
   Budapest, Ungarische Nationalgalerie

29. Leihhaus
   1874. Öl auf Leinwand, 165 × 240 cm
   New York, The Metropolitan Museum of Art

30. Maisfeld
   1874. Öl auf Holz, 67 × 102 cm
   Budapest, Ungarische Nationalgalerie

31. Staubiger Weg I.
   1874. Öl auf Holz, 77 × 117,5 cm
   Budapest, Ungarische Nationalgalerie

32. Staubiger Weg II.
   1874/83. Öl auf Holz, 96 × 129 cm
   Budapest, Ungarische Nationalgalerie

33. Esquisse pour le tableau A l'atelier *1875. Huile, bois, 50×60 cm* *Budapest, Galerie Nationale Hongroise*	33. Sketch for In the Studio *1875. Oil on wood, 50×60 cm* *Budapest, Hungarian National Gallery*	33. Im Atelier (Skizze) *1875. Öl auf Holz, 50×60 cm* *Budapest, Ungarische Nationalgalerie*
34. Étude pour le tableau Milton (Eve) *1877. Huile, toile, 56×46,5 cm* *Budapest, Galerie Nationale Hongroise*	34. Study for Milton (Eve) *1877. Oil on canvas, 56×46.5 cm* *Budapest, Hungarian National Gallery*	34. Studie zu Milton (Eva) *1877. Öl auf Leinwand, 56×46,5 cm* *Budapest, Ungarische Nationalgalerie*
35. Milton *1878. Huile, toile, 93×122 cm* *Budapest, Galerie Nationale Hongroise*	35. Milton *1878. Oil on canvas, 93×122 cm* *Budapest, Hungarian National Gallery*	35. Milton *1878. Öl auf Leinwand, 93×122 cm* *Budapest, Ungarische Nationalgalerie*
36. Portrait du cardinal Lajos Haynald *1884. Huile, bois, 116×89 cm* *Budapest, Galerie Nationale Hongroise*	36. Portrait of Cardinal Lajos Haynald *1884. Oil on wood, 116×89 cm* *Budapest, Hungarian National Gallery*	36. Porträt des Erzbischofs Lajos Haynald *1884. Öl auf Holz, 116×89 cm* *Budapest, Ungarische Nationalgalerie*
37. Intérieur parisien *1877. Huile, toile, 70,5×102 cm* *Budapest, Galerie Nationale Hongroise*	37. Paris Interior *1877. Oil on canvas, 70.5×102 cm* *Budapest, Hungarian National Gallery*	37. Pariser Interieur *1877. Öl auf Leinwand, 70,5×102 cm* *Budapest, Ungarische Nationalgalerie*
38. Intérieur parisien (détail)	38. Paris Interior (Detail)	38. Pariser Interieur (Ausschnitt)
39. Étude d'une baie *1877. Huile, bois, 64,5×53 cm* *Budapest, Galerie Nationale Hongroise*	39. Study of a Window-Recess *1877. Oil on wood, 64.5×53 cm* *Budapest, Hungarian National Gallery*	39. Fensternische (Studie) *1877. Öl auf Holz, 64,5×53 cm* *Budapest, Ungarische Nationalgalerie*
40. Le Lévrier *1882. Huile, toile, 81×105 cm* *Budapest, Galerie Nationale Hongroise*	40. The Hound *1882. Oil on canvas, 81×105 cm* *Budapest, Hungarian National Gallery*	40. Der Windhund *1882. Öl auf Leinwand, 81×105 cm* *Budapest, Ungarische Nationalgalerie*
41. Atelier (esquisse) *1876. Huile, toile, 45,3×63 cm* *Budapest, Galerie Nationale Hongroise*	41. Sketch for a Studio Interior *1876. Oil on canvas, 45.3×63 cm* *Budapest, Hungarian National Gallery*	41. Das Atelier (Skizze) *1876. Öl auf Leinwand, 45,3×63 cm* *Budapest, Ungarische Nationalgalerie*
42. Esquisse pour le tableau les Visiteurs de bébé *1879. Huile, bois, 36,5×48 cm* *Budapest, Galerie Nationale Hongroise*	42. Sketch for Baby's Visitors *1879. Oil on wood, 36.5×48 cm* *Budapest, Hungarian National Gallery*	42. Besuch bei der Wöchnerin (Skizze) *1879. Öl auf Holz, 36,5×48 cm* *Budapest, Ungarische Nationalgalerie*
43. Les Visiteurs de bébé *1879. Huile, bois, 140×149 cm* *Budapest, Galerie Nationale Hongroise*	43. Baby's Visitors *1879. Oil on wood, 140×149 cm* *Budapest, Hungarian National Gallery*	43. Besuch bei der Wöchnerin *1879. Öl auf Holz, 140×149 cm* *Budapest, Ungarische Nationalgalerie*
44. Les Visiteurs de bébé (détail)	44. Baby's Visitors (Detail)	44. Besuch bei der Wöchnerin (Ausschnitt)
45. Portrait de femme *1885. Huile, bois, 55×45 cm* *Budapest, Galerie Nationale Hongroise*	45. Woman's Portrait *1885. Oil on wood, 55×45 cm* *Budapest, Hungarian National Gallery*	45. Frauenporträt *1885. Öl auf Holz, 55×45 cm* *Budapest, Ungarische Nationalgalerie*
46. Esquisse pour le tableau la Mort de Mozart *1886. Huile, bois, 52×65 cm* *Budapest, Galerie Nationale Hongroise*	46. Sketch for The Death of Mozart *1886. Oil on wood, 52×65 cm* *Budapest, Hungarian National Gallery*	46. Mozarts Tod (Skizze) *1886. Öl auf Holz, 52×65 cm* *Budapest, Ungarische Nationalgalerie*
47. Nature morte avec fleurs et cruche *1881. Huile, toile, 106×139,5 cm* *Budapest, Galerie Nationale Hongroise*	47. Flower-Piece with Jug *1881. Oil on canvas, 106×139.5 cm* *Budapest, Hungarian National Gallery*	47. Blumenstilleben mit Krug *1881. Öl auf Leinwand, 106×139,5 cm* *Budapest, Ungarische Nationalgalerie*
48. Le Retour à la ferme *1882. Huile, toile, 216×198 cm* *Budapest, Galerie Nationale Hongroise*	48. Homewards *1882. Oil on canvas, 216×198 cm* *Budapest, Hungarian National Gallery*	48. Heimkehr *1882. Öl auf Leinwand, 216×198 cm* *Budapest, Ungarische Nationalgalerie*
49. Le Retour à la ferme (détail)	49. Homewards (Detail)	49. Heimkehr (Ausschnitt)

50. Grande Nature morte avec fleurs
1881. Huile, toile, 146,5×114,5 cm
Budapest, Galerie Nationale Hongroise

51. Le Troupeau au pâturage
1882. Huile, toile, 210×285 cm
Budapest, Galerie Nationale Hongroise

52. Campement de Bohémiens
1873. Huile, bois, 65×103 cm
Berlin, Nationalgalerie

53. Paysage avec lac
1881/82. Huile, bois, 46,5×56 cm
Budapest, Galerie Nationale Hongroise

54. Nature morte avec fleurs et plat
1882. Huile, bois, 55×42 cm
Budapest, Galerie Nationale Hongroise

55. Nature morte avec fleurs et plat (détail)

56. Allée
1880. Aquarelle, papier, 250×392 mm
Budapest, Galerie Nationale Hongroise

57. Station balnéaire
Vers 1890. Aquarelle, papier,
246×340 mm
Budapest, Galerie Nationale Hongroise

58. Allée et maison à étage
Vers 1883. Huile, bois, 49,5×61 cm
Budapest, Galerie Nationale Hongroise

59. Allée
1886. Huile, toile, 111,5×182 cm
Budapest, Galerie Nationale Hongroise

60. Allée (détail)

61. Le Parc de Colpach
1886. Huile, bois, 96×130,5 cm
Budapest, Galerie Nationale Hongroise

62. Étude pour le tableau le Christ
au prétoire
1880. Huile, toile, 82×65 cm
Budapest, Galerie Nationale Hongroise

63. Le Christ au prétoire
1881. Huile, toile, 124×218 cm
Budapest, Galerie Nationale Hongroise

64. Étude pour le tableau le Christ
au prétoire (Mère avec son enfant)
1880. Huile, bois, 64,5×52,5 cm
Budapest, Galerie Nationale Hongroise

65. Étude pour le Calvaire (arabe à cheval)
1882. Huile, toile, 150×110 cm
Budapest, Galerie Nationale Hongroise

66. Ecce homo
1895/96. Huile, toile, 403×650 cm
Debrecen, Musée Déri

50. Big Flower-Piece
1881. Oil on canvas, 146.5×114.5 cm
Budapest, Hungarian National Gallery

51. Cattle Grazing
1882. Oil on canvas, 210×285 cm
Budapest, Hungarian National Gallery

52. Gipsies (or Gipsy Camp)
1873. Oil on wood, 65×103 cm
Berlin, Nationalgalerie

53. Landscape with Lake
1881/82. Oil on wood, 46.5×56 cm
Budapest, Hungarian National Gallery

54. Flower-Piece with Bowl
1882. Oil on wood, 55×42 cm
Budapest, Hungarian National Gallery

55. Flower-Piece with Bowl (Detail)

56. Avenue
1880. Water colour on paper, 250×392 mm
Budapest, Hungarian National Gallery

57. Seaside Resort
About 1890. Water colour on paper,
246×340 mm
Budapest, Hungarian National Gallery

58. Avenue with House
1883. Oil on wood, 49.5×61 cm
Budapest, Hungarian National Gallery

59. Avenue
1886. Oil on canvas, 111.5×182 cm
Budapest, Hungarian National Gallery

60. Avenue (Detail)

61. The Park of Colpach
1886. Oil on wood, 96×130.5 cm
Budapest, Hungarian National Gallery

62. Study of Christ before Pilate
1880. Oil on canvas, 82×65 cm
Budapest, Hungarian National Gallery

63. Christ before Pilate
1881. Oil on canvas, 124×218 cm
Budapest, Hungarian National Gallery

64. Study for Christ before Pilate
(Mother and Child)
1880. Oil on wood, 64.5×52.5 cm
Budapest, Hungarian National Gallery

65. Study for Golgotha (Arab Horseman)
1882. Oil on canvas, 150×110 cm
Budapest, Hungarian National Gallery

66. Ecce Homo
1895/96. Oil on canvas, 403×650 cm
Debrecen, Déri Museum

50. Großes Blumenstilleben
1881. Öl auf Leinwand, 146,5×114,5 cm
Budapest, Ungarische Nationalgalerie

51. Weidende Herde
1882. Öl auf Holz, 210×285 cm
Budapest, Ungarische Nationalgalerie

52. Zigeunerlager
1873. Öl auf Holz, 65×103 cm
Berlin, Nationalgalerie

53. Landschaft mit See
1881/82. Öl auf Holz, 46,5×56 cm
Budapest, Ungarische Nationalgalerie

54. Blumenstilleben mit Schüssel
1882. Öl auf Holz, 55×42 cm
Budapest, Ungarische Nationalgalerie

55. Blumenstilleben mit Schüssel (Ausschnitt)

56. Allee
1880. Aquarell, Papier, 250×392 mm
Budapest, Ungarische Nationalgalerie

57. Am Meeresufer
Um 1890. Aquarell, Papier, 246×340 mm
Budapest, Ungarische Nationalgalerie

58. Allee mit einstöckigem Haus
Um 1883. Öl auf Holz, 49,5×61 cm
Budapest, Ungarische Nationalgalerie

59. Allee
1886. Öl auf Leinwand, 111,5×182 cm
Budapest, Ungarische Nationalgalerie

60. Allee (Ausschnitt)

61. Der Colpacher Park
1886. Öl auf Holz, 96×130,5 cm
Budapest, Ungarische Nationalgalerie

62. Christus vor Pilatus (Studie)
1880. Öl auf Leinwand, 82×65 cm
Budapest, Ungarische Nationalgalerie

63. Christus vor Pilatus
1881. Öl auf Leinwand, 124×218 cm
Budapest, Ungarische Nationalgalerie

64. Studie zu Christus vor Pilatus (Mutter
mit Kind)
1880. Öl auf Holz, 64,5×52,5 cm
Budapest, Ungarische Nationalgalerie

65. Studie zu Kreuzigung (Araberreiter)
1882. Öl auf Leinwand, 150×110 cm
Budapest, Ungarische Nationalgalerie

66. Ecce Homo
1895/96. Öl auf Leinwand, 403×650 cm
Debrecen, Déri-Museum

67. L'Apothéose de la Renaissance
1890.
Panneau de plafond au Kunsthistorisches
Museum de Vienne

68. Esquisse pour le tableau la Conquête
de la Hongrie
1892/93. Huile, toile, 210 × 625 cm
Szeged, Musée Móra Ferenc

69. La Grève
1895. Huile, toile, 159 × 251,5 cm
Budapest, Galerie Nationale Hongroise

70. Le parc Monceau la nuit
1895. Huile, toile, 130 × 200 cm
Budapest, Galerie Nationale Hongroise

67. The Apotheosis of the Renaissance
1890.
Ceiling panneau in the Kunsthistorisches
Museum, Vienna

68. Sketch for Árpád's Conquest of Hungary
1892/93. Oil on canvas, 210 × 625 cm
Szeged, Móra Ferenc Museum

69. Strike
1895. Oil on canvas, 159 × 251.5 cm
Budapest, Hungarian National Gallery

70. Parc Monceau at Night
1895. Oil on canvas, 130 × 200 cm
Budapest, Hungarian National Gallery

67. Apotheose der Renaissance
1890. Deckengemälde auf Leinwand im
Wiener Kunsthistorischen Museum

68. Landnahme (Skizze)
1892/93. Öl auf Leinwand, 210 × 625 cm
Szeged, Móra-Ferenc-Museum

69. Streik
1895. Öl auf Leinwand, 159 × 251,5 cm
Budapest, Ungarische Nationalgalerie

70. Parc Monceau am Abend
1895. Öl auf Leinwand, 130 × 200 cm
Budapest, Ungarische Nationalgalerie

1. Brigand affligé. 1865
   Woebegone Highwayman. 1865
   Trauernder Betyar. 1865

2. Orage sur la puszta. 1867
   Storm on the Puszta. 1867
   Gewitter auf der Pußta. 1867

3. Apprenti bâillant. 1869
   Yawning Apprentice. 1869
   Gähnender Lehrling. 1869

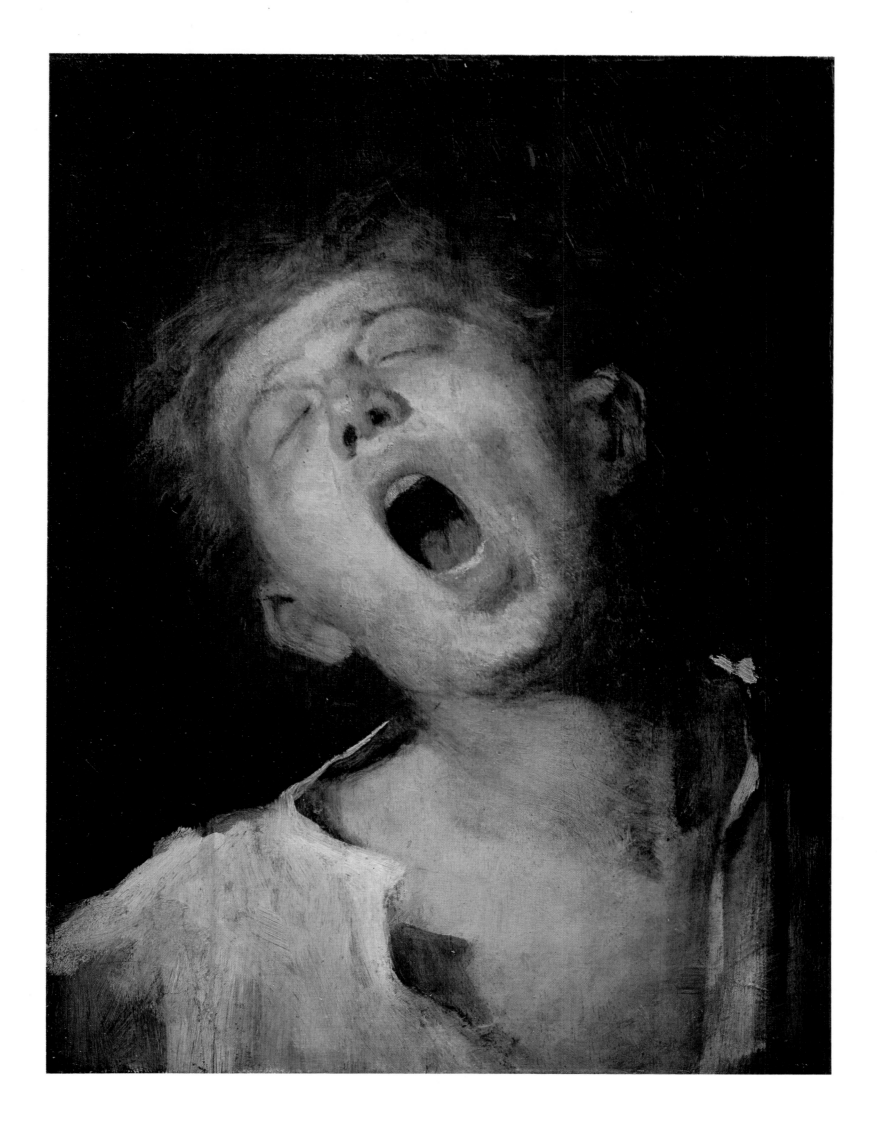

4. Le Dernier Jour d'un condamné. 1869
   The Condemned Cell. 1869
   Der letzte Tag eines Verurteilten. 1869

5. Portrait de la baronne de Marches. 1872/73
   Portrait of Baroness de Marches. 1872/73
   Porträt der Baronin de Marches. 1872/73

6. L'Instituteur de Colpach. 1882
   The Schoolmaster of Colpach. 1882
   Der Colpacher Lehrer. 1882

8. Faiseuses de charpie. 1871
   Lint Makers. 1871
   Scharpiezupferinnen. 1871

9. Coin de forêt. 1872
Forest Scene. 1872
Waldszene. 1872

10. Portrait de László Paál. 1877
Portrait of László Paál. 1877
Porträt des László Paál. 1877

11. La femme aux fagots. 1873
    Woman Carrying Faggots. 1873
    Reisigtragende Frau. 1873

12. La femme aux fagots (détail)
Woman Carrying Faggots (Detail)
Reisigtragende Frau (Ausschnitt)

14. Les Adieux. 1873
    Farewell. 1873
    Abschied. 1873

15. Pèlerin blessé. 1870/76
    Wounded Wanderer. 1870/76
    Der verwundete Wanderer. 1870/76

16. Sous l'auvent. 1869
Under the Eaves. 1869
Unter der Traufe. 1869

17. A la buanderie. 1877
    In the Laundry. 1877
    In der Waschküche. 1877

18. La rue sombre. 1871
    Dark Street. 1871
    Dunkle Gasse. 1871

19. A la taverne. Vers 1875
   In the Tavern. About 1875
   In der Schenke. Um 1875

20. Vagabonds de nuit. 1872/73
    Tramps of the Night. 1872/73
    Nächtliche Vagabunden. 1872/73

21. Vagabonds de nuit (détail)
   Tramps of the Night (Detail)
   Nächtliche Vagabunden (Ausschnitt)

22. Deux gars attablés
    (étude pour le tableau le Héros du village). 1874
    Two Youths at the Table
    (Study for The Hero of the Village). 1874
    Zwei Burschen am Tisch (Studie zu Dorfheld). 1874

23. Le Condamné. Vers 1872
    The Condemned. About 1872
    Der Verurteilte. Um 1872

24. Le Condamné (détail)
   The Condemned (Detail)
   Der Verurteilte (Ausschnitt)

25. Esquisse pour le tableau le Mont de Piété. 1871/73
    Sketch for The Pawnbroker's Shop. 1871/73
    Leihhaus (Skizze). 1871/73

26. Vieille femme assise
    (étude pour le tableau le Mont de Piété). 1873/74
    Seated Old Woman
    (Study for The Pawnbroker's Shop). 1873/74
    Sitzende alte Frau (Studie zu Leihhaus). 1873/74

27. Mère avec son enfant
(étude pour le tableau le Mont de Piété). 1873
Mother and Child
(Study for The Pawnbroker's Shop). 1873
Mutter mit Kind (Studie zu Leihhaus). 1873

28. L'Homme à la cape
(étude pour le tableau le Mont de Piété). 1874
Man in Coat (Study for The Pawnbroker's Shop). 1874
Mann mit Mantel (Studie zu Leihhaus). 1874

29. Le Mont de Piété. 1874
   The Pawnbroker's Shop. 1874
   Leihhaus. 1874

30. Le Champ de maïs. 1874
    The Maize-Field. 1874
    Maisfeld. 1874

33. Esquisse pour le tableau A l'atelier. 1875
Sketch for In the Studio. 1875
Im Atelier (Skizze). 1875

34. Étude pour le tableau Milton (Eve). 1877
    Study for Milton (Eve). 1877
    Studie zu Milton (Eva). 1877

35. Milton. 1878
Milton. 1878
Milton. 1878

36. Portrait du cardinal Lajos Haynald. 1884
   Portrait of Cardinal Lajos Haynald. 1884
   Porträt des Erzbischofs Lajos Haynald. 1884

37. Intérieur parisien. 1877
   Paris Interior. 1877
   Pariser Interieur. 1877

38. Intérieur parisien (détail)
Paris Interior (Detail)
Pariser Interieur (Ausschnitt)

39. Étude d'une baie. 1877
   Study of a Window-Recess. 1877
   Fensternische (Studie). 1877

40. Le Lévrier. 1882
The Hound. 1882
Der Windhund. 1882

42. Esquisse pour le tableau les Visiteurs de bébé. 1879
    Sketch for Baby's Visitors. 1879
    Besuch bei der Wöchnerin (Skizze). 1879

43. Les Visiteurs de bébé. 1879
    Baby's Visitors. 1879
    Besuch bei der Wöchnerin. 1879

44. Les Visiteurs de bébé (détail)
   Baby's Visitors (Detail)
   Besuch bei der Wöchnerin (Ausschnitt)

45. Portrait de femme. 1885
   Woman's Portrait. 1885
   Frauenporträt. 1885

46. Esquisse pour le tableau la Mort de Mozart. 1886
    Sketch to The Death of Mozart. 1886
    Mozarts Tod (Skizze). 1886

47. Nature morte avec fleurs et cruche. 1881
    Flower-Piece with Jug. 1881
    Blumenstilleben mit Krug. 1881

48. Le Retour à la ferme. 1882
    Homewards. 1882
    Heimkehr. 1882

51. Le Troupeau au pâturage. 1882
   Cattle Grazing. 1882
   Weidende Herde. 1882

52. Campement de Bohémiens. 1873
   Gipsies (or Gipsy Camp). 1873
   Zigeunerlager. 1873

53. Paysage avec lac. 1881/82
   Landscape with Lake. 1881/82
   Landschaft mit See. 1881/82

54. Nature morte avec fleurs et plat. 1882
Flower-Piece with Bowl. 1882
Blumenstilleben mit Schüssel. 1882

55. Nature morte avec fleurs et plat (détail)
Flower-Piece with Bowl (Detail)
Blumenstilleben mit Schüssel (Ausschnitt)

56. Allée. 1880
    Avenue. 1880
    Allee. 1880

58. Allée et maison à étage. Vers 1883
Avenue with House. About 1883
Allee mit einstöckigem Haus. Um 1883

59. Allée. 1886
   Avenue. 1886
   Allee. 1886

60. Allée (détail)
   Avenue (Detail)
   Allee (Ausschnitt)

61. Le Parc de Colpach. 1886
    The Park of Colpach. 1886
    Der Colpacher Park. 1886

62. Étude pour le tableau le Christ au prétoire. 1880
    Study for Christ before Pilate. 1880
    Christus vor Pilatus (Studie). 1880

63. Le Christ au prétoire. 1881
Christ before Pilate. 1881
Christus vor Pilatus. 1881

64. Étude pour le tableau le Christ au prétoire
   (Mère avec sont enfant). 1880
   Study for Christ before Pilate (Mother and Child). 1880
   Studie zu Christus vor Pilatus (Mutter mit Kind). 1880

65. Étude pour le Calvaire (Arabe à cheval). 1882
Study for Golgotha (Arab Horseman). 1882
Studie zu Kreuzigung (Araberreiter). 1882

66. Ecce homo. 1895/96
   Ecce homo. 1895/96
   Ecce Homo. 1895/96

67. L'Apothéose de la Renaissance. 1890
    The Apotheosis of the Renaissance. 1890
    Apotheose der Renaissance. 1890

68. Esquisse pour le tableau la Conquête de la Hongrie. 1892/93
Sketch for Árpád's Conquest of Hungary. 1892/93
Landnahme (Skizze). 1892/93

69. La Grève. 1895
Strike. 1895
Streik. 1895

70. Le parc Monceau la nuit. 1895
   Parc Monceau at Night. 1895
   Parc Monceau am Abend. 1895